IMAGES
of Sport

ST ANDREWS

AND ITS GOLFING LEGENDS

A postcard of Old Tom Morris, c. 1908.

IMAGES
of Sport

ST ANDREWS

AND ITS GOLFING LEGENDS

Compiled by
Stuart Marshall

TEMPUS

First published 2000
Copyright © Stuart Marshall, 2000

Tempus Publishing Limited
The Mill, Brimscombe Port,
Stroud, Gloucestershire, GL5 2QG

ISBN 0 7524 1812 2

Typesetting and origination by
Tempus Publishing Limited
Printed in Great Britain by
Midway Clark Printing, Wiltshire

Contents

Acknowledgements

Compiling this pictorial history has been both rewarding and fascinating. My thanks go to the schoolboys of yesteryear – without their habit of collecting I would not have been able to amass my collection, and in particular I wish to thank Imperial Tobacco for permission to reproduce many of those cards shown here.

Thanks are also due to Stuart Mackenzie, Jim Bone, Duncan Black, Jimmy Porter, Lettie Hirst, Bob Scully, Stephen Forrest of East Kilbride Golf Club, Eleanor Clark of the British Golf Museum, Matthew Jarron of the St Andrews Preservation Trust Museum, Carol Irvine for her patience in typing this book and lastly to my daughter – not only do we have the Open in 2000, but this is also the summer that she graduates from St Andrews with her docrorate in Physics as namely Dr Dawn Marshall.

Introduction

Golf in Scotland is supposed to have originated at St Andrews, where it was popular when the university was founded in 1413. In 1553 the Archbishop of St Andrews gave his approval and in 1608 James I of England (and VI of Scotland), who was a keen golfer, introduced it into England, where for 300 years it was played at Blackheath before spreading in popularity to the rest of the country.

In the early days golf was not a sport enjoyed by most of the population. Golf's progress was steady but yet extremely slow. However, as its popularity grew the professional element began to creep in. The early pros were those who looked after the condition of the courses and through practice in their spare time became skilled.

After a time it became customary to have a professional at every club, his duties being to look after the caddies and teach learners the game. Hence, two distinct groups evolved – the amateur and the professional – and, later, competitions which included either or both were inaugurated.

In 1860 Prestwick Golf Club began a competition for professionals with a prize of £5 and a Silver Belt. The following year amateurs were permitted to enter and it truly became 'open'. This Open Championship – better known as the British Open – was first won by Willie Park, who went on to win again in 1863 and 1866.

The Silver Belt became the property of Tom Morris junior, who won three times in succession in 1868, 1869 and 1870. The Championship went into abeyance for a year but was revived in 1872 when 'Young Tom' won again.

The Open Championship first came to St Andrews in 1873 and was won by Tom Kidd, who was the first to be awarded the cup or more correctly 'The Golf Champion Trophy'. In 1872 Young Tom had received a medal also titled 'The Golf Champion Trophy'.

Young Tom Morris' record of four successive wins has never been equalled yet two golfers achieved three successive wins, all within a period of six years: Jamie Anderson won in 1877, 1878 and 1879 and was immediately followed by Bob Ferguson in 1880, 1881 and 1882.

Between 1894 and 1900 two golfers dominated the Championship – J.H. Taylor and H. Vardon. They were joined in 1904 by J. Braid and they were called the 'triumvirate', a trio that was to dominate British golf for twenty years.

An Alphabet of St. Andrews

An interesting composition by the late Professor Crum Brown has been sent to us by a correspondent who is a keen student of the lore and literature of the game. Professorial golf has been, not with uniform fairness, summed up in the caddie's famous comment to the man of the Chair, "It tak's a heid to play gowff." Our correspondent reminds us that Professor Crum Brown was not a golfer "even in the limited professorial sense of the term, but he enjoyed great distinction at St. Andrews as the uncle of Freddy Tait."
Scotsman, 10th March, 1925.

A was his Attitude at the first tee.
B was the Burn he got into in three.
C was his Caddie, a little scapegrace.
D was the Divot he didn't replace.
E was the Energy rashly bestowed.
F was the Fore ! he roared out of the road.
G was the Globe that he missed with his putter ;
H was a Horrid word they heard him utter.
I was the Iron he used at the dyke ;
J was the Jerk laid him dead in the like.
K was a Kick knocked him into the nose ;
L was his Language which you may suppose,
M was his Mashie, he thought it would do ;
N was the Niblick he had to take too.
O was the Odd he played out of a whin.
P was a Putt he got cleverly in.
Q was a Quarrel arose unforseen, whether
R was or was not a Rub of the green.
S was a Stymie complete as could be ;
T was the Twist with which round it went he.
U was the Underspin makes the ball soar ;
V was the Velocity it should have been more.
W was Walkinshaw, he thought he had carried it ;
X was the Extra stroke after he'd buried it.
Y was the Yawning big bunker ahead ;
Z was the Zigzag he followed instead.
&c. Then comes " Et cetera " the rest of the round.
    You won't find an Alphabet for it I'll be bound.

Postcard from 1925.

One
St Andrews
The Town

Many golfers arrive at St Andrews little realising what an ancient and historic town they are visiting. The next few pages will set the scene to life in the days when local worthies such as Tom Morris and Alex Herd roamed the streets of the 'Old Town'.

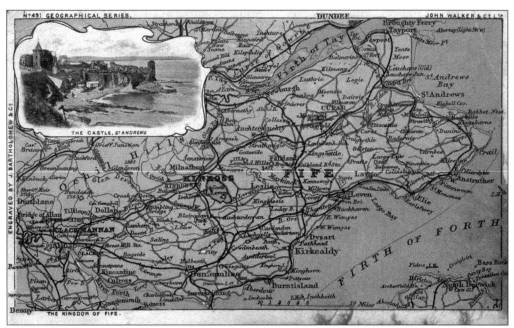

Postcard, *c.* 1908. St Andrews is the location of Scotland's oldest university, a historic cathedral town, a seaside resort and, above all it is the 'Home of Golf'.

This postcard shows the main part of the town with the Royal and Ancient clubhouse in the bottom right of the picture. Note the vacant spot just across the road where the British Golf Museum now stands.

Legend has it that the town of St Andrews came into being when the bones of Scotland's patron saint were brought here and buried in the church of St Regulus (also known as St Rule) over 1,000 years ago. Religion has always been prevalent within the community and the building of the cathedral in the twelfth century reaffirmed its importance.

The Town Church, St. Andrews.

St. ANDREWS.

Situated right in the centre of town on South Street, the town church is better known as Holy Trinity church, the local parish church for St Andrews. This postcard, from around 1905, incorporates the town crest.

ST.ANDREWS FROM NORTH.

207798.J.V.

Postcard, *c.* 1930. At the back of the picture, the cathedral and St Rule's Tower can clearly be seen. The main street leading up to these buildings is North Street.

ST. ANDREWS

THE HOME OF THE ROYAL AND ANCIENT GAME

ILLUSTRATED GUIDE FREE FROM TOWN CLERK OR ANY L·N·E·R OFFICE OR AGENCY

An advertising poster produced by the railway.

THE CROSS, MARKET STREET, ST. ANDREWS   73606. (JV)

This is where the Mercat Cross once stood – it has been replaced by a fountain. On bank holidays you can still find a small market here, including a book dealer from whom you can occasionally buy an old golf book or two!

CHARLES ROBERTSON,

CHEMIST and
PHOTOGRAPHIC DEALER.

High-Class Dispensing.   Purest Drugs and Chemicals.
Personal attention to all orders entrusted.
Photographic Goods in great variety.   Plates, Papers, Films, &c.
Plates and Films Developed—moderate charges.
Toilet Requisites.   Perfumes.   Soaps.   Skin Foods.
Tooth and Nail Brushes, Sponges, &c.

(NIGHT BELL.)

115, Market Street, - ST. ANDREWS.

Charles Robertson, c. 1903. The shop was at No. 115 Market Street.

The street where Tom Morris was born.

At the top of North Street near the cathedral is this restored house, now the St Andrews Preservation Trust Museum. This is a fascinating place to visit and, thanks to the curator, the source of some of the pictures in this book.

The three main streets in St Andrews all converge towards the cathedral, these being North Street, South Street and, in the middle, Market Street.

Another local retailer at the beginning of the twentieth century was J.W. MacArthur, a baker and confectioner situated at No. 34 South Street.

THE TENNIS COURTS, KINBURN PARK, ST. ANDREWS. B.4887.

Tennis is one of the many other sports to have also been played at the home of golf.

This picture from 1896 shows Ancient City Athletic, the junior team with a contradictory name: they were in fact older amateurs or semi-professionals. From left to right, back row: W.R. McKay (vice-president), J. Ripley, D. King, A. Adams (vice-captain), J. Mitchell, R. Nicholson. Middle row: W. Grant, D. Harvey, R. Mitchell (captain), J. Lees, C. King. Front row: J. Lothian, W. King, P. Walker, J. Rae, H. Williamson.

An early postcard, *c.* 1900. Its title (on the reverse) reads 'First Class Family and Commercial Omnibus meets the train'.

Postcard, *c.* 1901. After William IV became patron of the Royal and Ancient in 1834, golfers began to arrive at St Andrews in vast numbers. Hotels like The Grand, now a university residence, and the equally massive Rusacks were packed with enthusiastic golfers.

213645.J.V.   THE HARBOUR, ST. ANDREWS.

St Rules Tower and the eastern end of what was once St Andrews Cathedral can be seen in the background of this picture postcard.

Wills's Cigarettes.

Arms of University of St. Andrews.

The University of St Andrews was founded in 1410 by Lawrence Lindores, the Abbot of Scone. There are three separate constituent colleges to the institution: the United Colleges of St Salvador (1450), St Leonard's (1512) and St Mary's College (1537).

S 1220 ON THE SANDS, ST. ANDREWS

For holidaymakers there are golden sands, deep blue seas, boating, fishing, sun-bathing, tennis, bowls, cinema, delightful walks and, of course, for the less energetic there's always golf.

On the Sands, St. Andrews

At the turn of the century pierrots would travel the country giving shows at various seaside towns. Both of the two postcards no this page are from around 1908.

This postcard was posted on 6 August 1903. It shows the northern end of South Street, which was once the main entrance to the Old City of St Andrews.

These suppliers of 'all golfing requisites' were situated at No. 117 South Street. This advertisement was placed in a rare golfing handbook produced in 1903.

Postcard, *c.* 1908. The Martyrs' Monument is sited close to Witch Hill, where women suspected of being witches were burnt. The monument commemorates those who died at the stake before the Reformation in 1559.

THE MARTYRS MONUMENT AND R. & A. GOLF CLUB HOUSE, ST. ANDREWS. B.337

Postcard, *c.* 1930.

ST. ANDREWS, FIFE

St Andrews castle, the construction of which began in 1200. This was the main residence and fortress for the bishops of St Andrews. This cigarette card was issued by W.A. & A.C. Churchman in 1938. The set of 48 is called 'Holiday Homes in Britain'.

THE ENTRANCE, ST. ANDREWS CASTLE

Postcard, c. 1906. John Knox took refuge here in 1547. Many sieges occurred and the castle was often in English hands.

On this and the next page are some more photographs of local businesses at the beginning of the twentieth century.

E. Walker's was sited on Bell Street, which runs between Market Street and South Street, and still has some nice shops.

E. WALKER,

13, Bell Street,
ST. ANDREWS.

Stationery, Artists' Materials, Photographs, Post-Cards, Souvenirs, &c., &c.

Original Pictures in Oil and Water-Colour always on view.

JOHN FRAME,

Grocer and - -
Wine Merchant.

Has always on hand a Well-selected Stock of the FINEST GROCERIES & PROVISIONS, which are retailed at Lowest Market Prices.

BURTON BEER & LONDON STOUT
Always in Prime Condition.

BURGOYNE'S BURGUNDIES.

All the leading Special Whiskies stocked.

43, Argyle Street,
ST. ANDREWS.

John Frame, grocer and wine merchant of Argyle Street, which is joined to South Street at the West Port. The picture for the postcard on page 20 could almost have been taken from the front of this shop.

Ellice Place is just off North Street, close to the cinema.

Thomas Evans, fishmonger and oyster dealer of Church Street, which lies between Market Street and South Street, close to the public library.

Two
The Royal and Ancient

The 'R&A', as it is affectionately known, is the governing body of the game. Founded in 1754, under the title of the St Andrews Golf Club, it was granted the title 'Royal and Ancient' in 1834 by King William IV. The present clubhouse was erected in 1840. Pictured above is the Union Parlour, the first R&A clubhouse, located where the Grand Hotel was later constructed. This photograph from around 1848 is courtesy of the St Andrews Preservation Trust Museum.

Manager, A. J. HITCHMAN.   GRAND HOTEL, ST. ANDREWS.

This is the site of the original clubhouse (it is now a university residence). The writer of this postcard in 1908 states that 'The hotel is very comfortable and full'.

R. & A. GOLF CLUB HOUSE, ST. ANDREWS.   216108

Although the R&A is possibly the most prestigious club in the world it is not the oldest. Three earlier organisations are Royal Blackheath (founded 1608), The Royal Burgess Golfing Society of Edinburgh (1735) and the Honourable Company of Edinburgh Golfers (1744).

Motorists outside New Club, *c.* 1910. The R&A clubhouse lies to the left of the upper end of Golf Place.

Postcard, *c.* 1906. Note Old Tom Morris with his hand on the flag.

18TH GREEN AND R. & A. CLUB HOUSE, ST. ANDREWS.   B.856.

This page features two postcards from the 1930s. The eighteenth hole is named after Old Tom Morris.

THE 18TH GREEN, OLD COURSE, ST. ANDREWS.   B.3381.

To quote Winston Churchill: 'Golf is a game whose aim is to hit a very small ball into an even smaller hole, with weapons singularly ill-designed for that purpose.'

Postcard, *c*. 1930, looking from the links in a southerly direction.

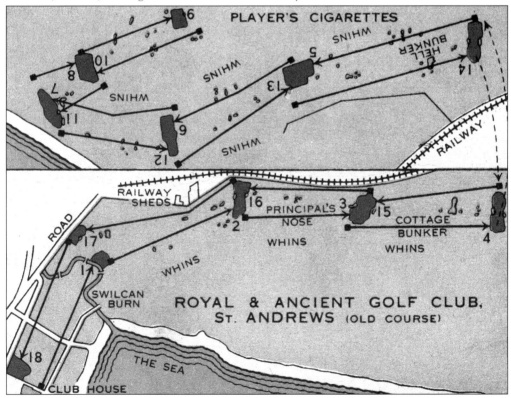

Issued in 1936, this is No. 1 in a series of 25 cards titled 'Championship Golf Courses'.

This cigarette card from 1924 was No. 21 of 25 in a set entitled 'Golfing'.

GOLF.

A Weekly Record of "ye Royal and Auncient" Game.

"Far and Sure."

No. 1. Vol. 1.]   FRIDAY, SEPTEMBER 19TH, 1890.   *Price Twopence.*
10s. 6d. per Annum, Post Free.

Fixtures.

ROYAL AND ANCIENT GOLF CLUB OF
ST. ANDREWS.—FIXTURES, 1890.

AUTUMN MEETING.

The Business Meeting will take place on Tuesday, 23rd September, at 5 p.m.
The Silver Club, the Royal or King William IV. Medal, the Royal Adelaide Medal, and the Gold Medal of the Club will be competed for on Wednesday, 24th September. Entries close on Tuesday, 23rd September, at 5 p.m.
The Annual Ball will take place on the evening of Thursday, 25th September.

SEPTEMBER.

Sept. 20.—Alnmouth ; Mr. Tod-Heatley's Prize.
Sept. 21.—Alnmouth ; Handicap Cup.
Sept. 27.—Luffness ; President's Medal and Mr. Tait's Star. Buxton and High Peak ; Competition for Medal ; also Handicap Sweepstake.
Littlehampton ; Mr. A. J. Constable's Medal.

OCTOBER.

Oct. 4, 5, 6.—Alnmouth ; Autumn Meeting.
Oct. 4, 7, 8, 10.—Royal North Devon ; Autumn Meeting.
Oct. 4.—Clapham ; " Cronin " Medal.
St. Nicholas, Prestwick ; Bailie Watson's Medal.
Oct. 7, 8, 9.—North Berwick ; Amateur Golf Tournament. Carnoustie and Taymouth ; Sweepstake Competition.
Oct. 8.—Royal Liverpool ; Autumn Meeting.
Oct. 11.—Tantallon Autumn Meeting ; Club Medal, Victoria Jubilee Cup.
St. George's (Sandwich) ; Autumn Meeting.
Oct. 13.—Royal Isle of Wight ; Autumn Meeting.
Oct. 18.—Ashdown Forest and Tunbridge Wells. Clapham ; Autumn Meeting.
Oct. 25.—Luffness ; Wemyss Challenge Handicap Medal. Buxton and High Peak ; Monthly Competition, under Handicap, with Sweepstake.
Oct. 26.—Alnmouth ; Final Competition for Handicap Cup.

NOVEMBER.

Nov. 1.—Great Yarmouth ; Autumn Meeting. Carnoustie and Taymouth ; Sweepstake Competition. Clapham ; " Cronin " Medal.
Nov. 4.—Great Yarmouth and Cambridge University ; at Yarmouth.
Nov. 29.—Royal Liverpool ; St. Andrews Meeting. Buxton and High Peak ; Monthly Competition, under Handicap, and Sweepstake.
Royal Isle of Wight ; St. Andrews Meeting.

DECEMBER.

Dec. 6.—Clapham ; " Cronin " Medal.
Dec. 23.—Royal Isle of Wight Christmas Meeting.
Dec. 26.—Bembridge Gold Medal, Eaton Memorial Putter and Fisher Prize.
Clapham ; Challenge Handicap Cup.
Dec. 27.—Buxton and High Peak ; Monthly Competition, under Handicap, with Sweepstake.

JANUARY.

Jan. 18.—Royal Epping Forest Golf Club, Quarterly Meeting and Monthly Competition.

To Golfers!

SURELY no apology is necessary for bringing before the public a weekly journal devoted to the doings and sayings of golfers, both past and present.

The extension of what has been justly termed the National Game of Scotland has made such rapid strides in the last few years, that there is hardly a place of any notoriety in the British Islands, and in India and many of the Colonies, that does not boast of its Golfing Green, either in its immediate vicinity, or, within easy reach ; and yet, although it is a game in which more interest is taken than in any other pastime, with the exception perhaps of Cricket and Football, there is at present no journal in existence which makes the "Royal and Ancient" and now popular Game its principal subject of attention.

Our object is to supply this great want. As we cannot possibly clash with any other interest, and as we have been promised the support of many of the "learned and witty" of our golfing brethren, we boldly and unhesitatingly launch our "bonny bark" on that "happy sea" which is now crowded by sailors, whose distinguishing feature has been, and we trust may long continue to be, that of "GOOD FELLOWSHIP."

ST. ANDREWS, N.B.

RUSACK'S HOTEL, MARINE ᴏʀ ᴛʜᴇ LINKS,

The Golf Metropolis—Parties Boarded.

SPECIAL TERMS TO GOLFERS & FAMILIES.

N. RUSACK, Proprietor and Manager.

Telegrams : RUSACK, St. ANDREWS, N.B.   Telephone No. 1011.

A weekly newspaper of sixteen pages. You would need good eyesight to read the very small print. This was the first issue and originally retailed at tuppence.

Three
Royalty

H.R.H. THE PRINCE OF WALES AT ST. ANDREWS.
"PLAYING HIMSELF IN" AS CAPTAIN OF THE R. & A. GOLF CLUB.

DUNDEE ADVERTIS
PHOTO

A postcard featuring the Prince of Wales, later to become Edward VIII, who was an active captain of the R&A. He was so popular he was made a Freeman of the City. Pictured here in 1922, a crowd of over 7,000 turned up to watch him being 'played-in' as captain.

AT WALTON HEATH

THE LIFE OF H.M. KING EDWARD VIII

A SERIES OF 50

23

AT WALTON HEATH

When the King gave up hunting in 1926, he turned to golf for relaxation. Before this, in 1922, His Majesty had publicly played himself in as Captain of the Royal and Ancient Golf Club at St. Andrews, the governing body of golf. " An awful job " was how he described this occasion when he discovered that all St. Andrews had assembled at 8 a.m. to watch the ceremony. In 1932, with a handicap of 11, the King reached the semi-final of the Parliamentary Golf Handicap at Walton Heath. In the following year he was in the final of the Parliamentary Tournament.

W. D. & H. O. WILLS

This is card number 23 from the rare, withdrawn set by W.D. & H.O. Wills called 'The Life of His Majesty King Edward VIII'. Due to Edward's abdication the set was withdrawn and only a few escaped into circulation.

Of course Royalty has long been associated with golf. Mary Queen of Scots and her son James VI of Scotland (James I of England 1603-1625) were both extremely keen players. Even within days of the murder of her husband Lord Darnley, Mary was seen playing golf.

126
MARY, QUEEN OF SCOTS
Daughter of James V. Born 7 Dec., 1542.
Beheaded at Fotheringay, 8 Feb., 1587.

PHOTO. NEURDIN.

Ogden's *Guinea Gold Cigarettes.*

19.—CHARLES I.
A Royal and Ancient Golfer.

From 1502-1688 all the reigning monarchs were golfers. This cigarette card of Charles I is taken from a Cope Brothers set entitled 'Cope's Golfers' issued around 1900.

King George VI was an avid golfer. This cigarette card was distributed by Ardath tobacco just a few years after he was elected captain of the R&A.

125.F.   THE ROYAL AND ANCIENT GAME OF GOLF. BEAGLES' POSTCARDS.
          H.R.H. PRINCE ALBERT.

The Duke of Windsor's (King Edward VIII) full name was Albert Edward Christian George Andrew Patrick David Windsor. This postcard, from around 1910, refers to him as Prince Albert, although he was more commonly known as the Prince of Wales. He started to play golf at fourteen years of age so this postcard must be one of the earliest recordings of his golfing career, which included being first president of the Boy's Golf Championship Committee.

Four
The Old Course

Looking from the left of the clubhouse, *c.* 1930.

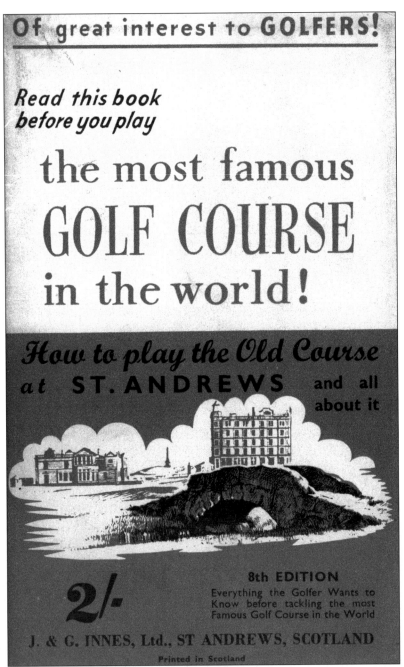

Of great interest to GOLFERS!

*Read this book
before you play*

the most famous
GOLF COURSE
in the world!

How to play the Old Course
at ST. ANDREWS and all about it

2/-

8th EDITION
Everything the Golfer Wants to Know before tackling the most Famous Golf Course in the World

J. & G. INNES, Ltd., ST ANDREWS, SCOTLAND

Printed in Scotland

Bobby Jones stated: 'St Andrews is the most fascinating golf course I have ever played. When I first played there in 1921, I was unable to understand the reverence with which the place was regarded by our British friends. I considered St Andrews among the very worst courses I had ever seen … In the interim between 1921 and my next visit to Britain in 1926, I heard such a great deal of St Andrews from Tommy Armour and other Scotsmen that I was determined to make an effort to like it. I really did not have to try very hard. Before I had played two rounds, I loved it, and I love it now.' Published by the *St Andrews Citizen*, a weekly newspaper, this forty-four page booklet told you all that you needed to know about the course.

The photograph for this postcard was taken from the corner of Grannie Clark's Wynd and The Links in 1937.

The Home Hole, from here to the eighteenth green. 'The Links' is the name of the street on the right. Further up is where Old Tom Morris had his shop (see page 57).

COPYRIGHT PHOTO BY ST ANDREWS LINKS, DRIVING TO 18TH HOLE. JAMES PATRICK

Having beautiful weather we had a lot of visitors staying with us E F B

This card was posted in 1904 to a Miss Hunter living at Westerleas, Murrayfield, Edinburgh.

THE FAMOUS ROAD HOLE, ST. ANDREWS.

This card was posted in 1938.

St Andrews. From 16th Hole Tee. Showing corner of Dyke and sheds to be cleared. Length 456 yds. (5 Hole)

The sheds referred to in the postcard belonged to the railway and this is now the site of the Old Course Hotel.

St Andrews. On the 4th Hole Green. Length of Hole 385 yds. (4 Hole)

This postcard probably features the 1905 Open at St Andrews, the winner being James Braid with Rowland Jones second.

This card was posted on 29 November 1913.

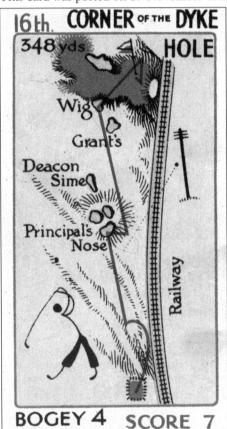

16th. CORNER OF THE DYKE HOLE
348 yds.

Wig
Grant's
Deacon Sime
Principal's Nose
Railway

BOGEY 4   SCORE 7

CAN YOU BEAT BOGEY AT ST. ANDREWS ?
SERIES OF 55   CARD NO. 48

MR. RABBIT'S ROUND—16TH HOLE.

There is nothing more frightening than a railway, and Mr. Rabbit would certainly have been in it if his ball had not hit a telegraph post and come back nearly to where it started. His second was in the Principal's Nose and he had to get out sideways. His fourth was too much to the left and in the Wig, where he had been about two hours and a half before. "Now for a long putt" he said hopefully, after his niblick shot, but he did not get it. **7.**

Bernard Darwin

For Particulars of a Competition in connection with this card, see the inset enclosed with this packing.
W. A. & A. C. CHURCHMAN, IPSWICH.
Issued by The Imperial Tobacco Company (of Great Britain and Ireland), Limited.

Churchman cigarettes issued this set of fifty-five cards called 'Can You Beat Bogey at St Andrews' in 1934. The most sought after card in this set is the last one, which can be found in at least three designs – all of which are joker cards featuring a bottle of whisky to signify the 'nineteenth hole'.

Golfing.—In a Bunker
St Andrews.

When in a Bunker, don't despair,
Wield well your club. Ball flies in air. yours.

A view looking northwards at the beginning of the twentieth century. Ed Furgol, an American professional, once rather unkindly remarked that 'There is nothing wrong with St Andrews that a hundred bulldozers couldn't put right'. This card was posted in 1903.

Postcard, *c.* 1910. The Old Course was initially over twenty-two holes before it was reduced to eighteen, due in no small measure to William St Clair, who totalled 121 over the original course.

VALENTINES SERIES

Golfing.—A Disputed Shot

When o'er this trackless moor
your're played,
Wherein the ball doth roam,
your thoughts will soon onot be on Golf
But on retaining home.

This page features two more postcards from the turn of the century. The old town of St Andrews can be seen far right in the background on this image. Legend has it that Sam Snead, on first seeing St Andrews, said 'Say, that looks like an old abandoned golf course. What do they call it?'

VLENTINES SERIES

Golfing.—A Difficult Shot

We shall
be very
pleased
to come
on Wedn
at 4 o'c
& C.

really
vicarage

At one time women were allowed to bleach clothes on the course – they had to get the water from somewhere! In 1842 the rules stated: 'When a ball lies on clothes, or within a club-length of a washing tub, the clothes may be drawn from under the ball and the tub may be removed.'

It is difficult to know exactly where this photograph was taken. In the background, on the far right, are the Black Sheds (railway sidings) and in the centre of the background is the goods yard (now the Old Course Hotel). The picture was taken across the course with the sea behind the photographer's left shoulder. Who says it never rains in St Andrews?

Golfing.—The Swing

Two instructional postcards on the Old Course, *c*. 1900.

VALENTINES SERIES

SCOTTISH S. JOES

Golfing.—"The Swing"

Will be down with the 6.15 from St. Enoch
Same as B.S. I.T.Mc.T.

Before 1901 it was illegal to write anything other than the address on the back of a postcard. Hence postcard publishers would leave blank spaces at the side or bottom of each card for a message or greeting to be scribbled there.

Golfing.—Among the Whins

Another pair of cards showing golfing life in the early days – you had to watch out for the sheep and rabbits!

Golf.—"Putting."

The R&A clubhouse can be seen in the background of this image.

Postcards from pictures, *c.* 1880. Old Daw used to sell milk and fruit refreshments from his barrow, usually located near Swilken Bridge.

Old Tom Morris pictured enjoying a glass of milk.

Top: Postcard featuring the Long Hole, *c.* 1920. *Middle:* Bobby Jones putting at the seventeenth surrounded by a huge crowd. *Right:* Card 51 from Churchmans 'Can You Beat Bogey at St Andrews?'

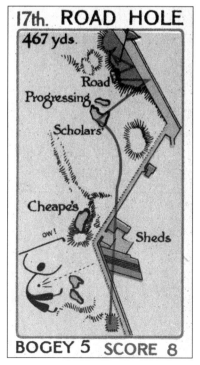

Originally sent in 1931, this postcard shows where the author goes when the Old Course proves too much!

A 1920s postcard by British Rail.

Five

St Andrews
Open Winners
1873-1939

CHAMPIONS OF THE BRITISH OPEN

In 1868 young Tom Morris won his first open, beating his father and eight other golfers at prestwick the venue of the first 12 opens.
In 1870 young Tom won for a third time and the organisers stipulated that for this achievement he was to keep the belt.

This and the following three pages are from a set of sixty-eight trade cards of the Open Champions, produced by David Foster in conjunction with the *Liverpool Post and Echo* at the 1998 Open Championship at Royal Birkdale.

Left: Tom Kidd, 1873: score 179. Winner of the first St Andrew's Open (runner-up was Jamie Anderson. *Right:* Bob Martin, Open winner in 1876 and 1885.

Left: Jamie Anderson, Open winner in 1879. He also won the Open in 1887 (Musselburgh) and in 1878 (Prestwick). *Right:* Robert Ferguson, holder of a hat-trick of wins, in 1882 as well as in 1880 (Musselburgh) and 1881 (Prestwick).

Left: Jack Burns, 1888: score 171. Runners-up Ben Sayers and David Anderson. *Right:* John Taylor, 1895 and 1900. Also champion in 1894 (Sandwich) and 1904 (Deal).

Left: Hugh Kirkaldy, 1891: score 166. Runners-up Andrew Kirkaldy (his brother) and Willie Fernie. *Right:* James Braid, 1905 and 1910. Also the winner in 1901, 1906 (both Muirfield) and 1908 (Prestwick).

Left: Jack Hutchinson, 1921: score 296. He won a play-off against Roger Wethered. Although born in St Andrews he later became an American citizen. *Right:* Bobby Jones, 1927. Also a champion in 1926 (Royal Lytham) and 1930 (Hoylake).

Left: Denny Shute, 1933: score 292. Runner-up was Craig Wood. *Right:* Richard Burton, 1936: score 290. Runner-up was Johnny Bulla.

Six

The Morrises

FOUNDER OF FIRM

TOM MORRIS

CHAMPION 1861-62, 64, 67

SON OF FOUNDER.

TOM MORRIS, JUNR.
(YOUNG TOMMY)

CHAMPION 1868-69, 70, 72.

WINNER OF CHAMPIONSHIP BELT AND 1st CHAMPIONSHIP MEDAL

RECORD ST. ANDREWS COURSE. 1869 77 STROKES

Tom Morris (senior), a magnificent golfer, was held in the highest esteem, not only for his golfing prowess but also for his cheery disposition. A real St Andrews golfing legend, he was born in the town on 16 June 1821. Old Tom won the won the Open in 1861, 1862, 1864 and 1867. He was known as 'Old Tom' to distinguish him from his son 'Young Tom', also an excellent golfer, who died tragically young. This postcard dates from around 1903 and is one of the most popular of the two Morrises.

A splendid postcard of Old Tom Morris.

Tom Morris.   Champion 1861. 1862. 1864. 1867.

The Wrench Series, No. 2006

St. Andrews.   The Golf Club House

The Wrench Series, No. 2039

This postcard, from around 1907, shows Old Tom on the home green which is named after him.

2.—TOM MORRIS.
The G.O.M. of Golf.

Left: Old Tom acting as caddy to Colonel J.O. Fairlee, who was a member of the R&A from 1838 and captain of the club in 1850. *Right*: 'Cope's Golfers' cigarette card. Note that 'G.O.M.' stands for 'Grand Old Man'.

As ever, Old Tom was always ready to help others, as this postcard from around 1901 demonstrates.

OLD TOM

Another postcard of Old Tom, who first started to play golf at the age of six. Also known as the 'First Architect of Golf', he helped to lay many courses, including Muirfield, Prestwick, Cheltenham and Westward Ho!

Tom Morris.

Ogden's *Guinea Gold Cigarettes*

Ogden cigarettes gave away many golfers amongst their series. This particular example from the 'Guinea Gold' series is a fine specimen and dates from around 1900.

A picture of Old Tom's Golf Shop as it is now.

This is the view that he would have seen as he stood in the doorway of his shop.

Father and son: Old and Young Tom Morris. Although born in St Andrews, Young Tom learned most of his golf at Prestwick where his father was greenkeeper. Young Tom turned professional at sixteen and won the Open in 1868, 1869, 1870 and 1872. His first three wins allowed him to keep the Belt – but also meant that there was no Championship in 1871.

Young Tom did not live long as he was found dead of a burst blood vessel on Christmas Day 1875, aged just twenty-four. Less than a year before this, his wife had died giving birth (the child also died). This exceptionally gifted but incredibly unfortunate man was the great tragic figure of nineteenth-century golf.

26. —TOM MORRIS, JNR.

Seven
The Early Days

1. W. Fernie.
2. H. Vardon.
3. J. Braid.
4. J. Taylor.
5. C. H. May
6. A. Simpson
7. J. White.
8. A. Herd.
9. A. Kirkald
10. B. Sayers, Ju
11. J. H. Tayl
12. A. Massey
13. G. Duncan

This postcard, from around 1905, epitomises all that is good in golf. The following pages illustrate just a few of the famous people – not always famous purely for their golf – who have graced St Andrews with their presence from the early days to 1940. Every one of them is a golfing legend.

Pictured outside the R&A clubhouse in 1857, this group of golfers were gathering for the Grand National Interclub Tournament.

CHURCHMAN'S CIGARETTES.

THE OPEN CHAMPIONSHIP CUP

CHURCHMAN'S CIGARETTES

THE AMATEUR CHAMPIONSHIP CUP.

In the years to come many of these golfers would be competing for these two trophies, reproduced here from Churchman's 1927 'Sporting Trophies' set.

Willie Park Junior won the 1887
Open, but at St Andrews the
following year he finished
eleventh. Regaining the title in
1889, he competed in the St
Andrews Open in 1885, 1891 and
1900 – finishing fifth, sixth and
sixth respectively.

A golfing postcard produced from a photograph taken around the 1850s. From left to right:
James Wilson (clubmaker), Bob Andrew (The Rook), Willie Dunn, Willie Park, Allan
Robertson, D. Anderson (Daw), Tom Morris and Bob Kirk.

The year 1839 saw the emergence of Allan Robertson. Born in 1815, he was a St Andrews man through and through and died in 1858.

Such was Robertson's ability that at the R&A Autumn meeting of 1842 he was 'prohibited by his brethren from competing' – the reasoning behind this was that his superior skill did not allow anyone else a chance. This picture comes from the 'Cope's Golfers' series.

12.—ALLAN ROBERTSON.

Charles Hutchings was a member of the R&A, Buxton and Pau golf clubs. He took up golf at the age of thirty and won the Amateur Championship in 1902 when a grandfather. He was the winner of many St Andrews competitions, including the Jubilee Vase in 1894.

Bernard Sayers was born in Leith in 1857. Although only 5ft 4ins tall, he was able to hold his own in all aspects of the game. Sayers played in every Open Championship from 1880 until 1923. At the St Andrews Championship of 1888 he achieved his highest ever finish, coming second to Jack Burns.

Andrew Kirkaldy was born in Denhead, just outside St Andrews, in 1860. An excellent golfer even in his youth, he was a well-known St Andrews professional. At the 1889 Open final he tied with Willie Park but lost on the replay. Kirkaldy died in St Andrews on 16 April 1934.

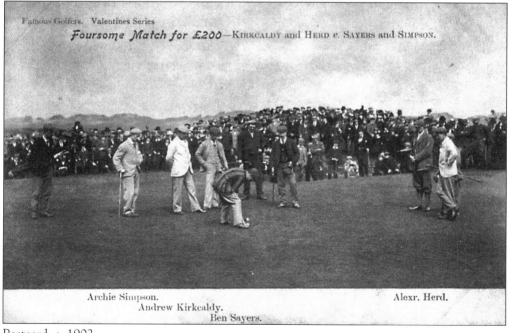

Postcard, *c.* 1902.

Mr. Mure Fergusson.   Mr. J. E. Laidlay.

The Wrench Series, No. 1984

S. Mure Ferguson was a keen R&A member, winning the King William IV Medal in St Andrews in 1874, 1881, 1886, 1888, 1893 and 1897. Ferguson was also the winner of the Gold Medal in 1877 and in 1895 finished as runner-up to John Ball in the 1894 Amateur Championship.

27.—J. E. LAIDLAY.

J.E. Laidley was another R&A member who twice won the Amateur Championship, the first win coming at St Andrews in 1889. Laidley also came tenth in the 1880 St Andrews Open. The picture is from a 'Cope's Golfers' cigarette card of around 1900.

Horace G. Hutchison was a member of the R&A as well as numerous other clubs. When the 'first' Amateur Championship was held at St Andrews in 1886 he emerged as the winner (later this was amended to the second championship). A prolific writer of books, which included *The Book of Golf* and *Golf 1899*, he became the first Englishman to be appointed captain of the R&A in 1908 and was a member of the Rules of Golf Committee.

21.—H. G. HUTCHINSON.
Literary Golf Champion.

9.—ANDREW LANG.
" The Laureate of Golf."

Andrew Lang was a poet, writer and genuine St Andrews man. He is buried in the Eastern cemetery near the Holy Well – virtually behind Young Tom Morris's monument. Regarded as a genius of his day, this enthusiastic golfer was a member of the R&A and, like Horace G. Hutchinson, is illustrated here in the 'Cope's Golfers' series of around 1900.

This card was posted in St Andrews on 4 April 1904. Robert Maxwell won the Amateur Championship in 1903 and 1909, also representing Scotland eight times between 1902 and 1910. He won the Royal Medal in 1901 and 1903, and the Gold Medal in 1902 and 1909. This postcard could well have been sent when he won the Silver Cross, the first prize at the Spring meeting, in 1904.

Tom Morris.   Mr H. H. Hilton.   Mr J. L. Low.

Famous Golfers. Valentines Series   *Amateur Championship.*

Harold Hilton won the Amateur Championship at St Andrews in 1901 and 1911.

As well as the St Andrews Amateur Championships of 1901 and 1911, Hilton won the Open Championship in 1892 and 1897; the Amateur Championship in 1900 and 1913; the Trustee Championship in 1891, 1900, 1901 and 1902; and the St Georges Vase in 1893 and 1894. He was a prolific writer and the first editor of *Golf Monthly*. Born in 1819, he was small in build but extremely powerful and died on 5 March 1942.

24.—HAROLD HILTON.

Edward Blackwell and F.G. Tait about to start a medal round in September 1899. Edward Baird Hay Blackwell, an R&A member, won both the King William IV Medal and the R&A Club Medal in 1892, the latter competition again in 1907, as well as the Silver Cross in 1902, 1903 and 1906 and the Victoria Jubilee Vase in 1903 – not to mention a host of other competitions! He was runner-up in the 1904 Amateur Championship.

Postcard, *c.* 1906. John Taylor won five Open Championships. In three of them the runners-up were the others in this card: 1895, St Andrews (Alex Herd); 1900, St Andrews (Harry Vardon); 1909, Deal (James Braid).

Taken a few years on from the postcard above, this photograph shows Taylor (middle seated), Vardon (second from left standing) and Alex Herd (second from right standing).

JAMES BRAID

James Braid was born in Earlsferry (Fife) on 6 February 1870. He began golfing as an amateur before becoming professional in 1896. He was a winner of the Open five times, including at St Andrews in 1905 and 1910. He served an apprenticeship as a joiner and later became a respected maker of golf clubs. This cigarette card comes from the set of twenty-seven by J. Millhoff issued in 1928.

Probably one of the greatest ever Scotsmen, Braid died on 27 November 1950.

Above left: 'Scotland's Own' played a very good game of golf and was a frequent visitor to St Andrews. *Above right*: The name Melville is synonymous with golf and St Andrews. There is little doubt that when he was rector of St Andrews University in 1590 he took advantage of the links.

From the 'Cope's Golfers' series, this card is based on the Revd Kerr, who liked nothing better than a trip to St Andrews. He was famous for his books on both golf and curling.

Mr John Ball. The late Mr F. G. Tait,
Amateur Championship.

Famous Golfers.   Valentines Series

John Ball became the first amateur to win the Open in 1890. He was Amateur Champion eight times between 1888 and 1912. At the age of fifteen he competed in the 1876 Open and finished sixth. Born in December 1861, he died in December 1940.

25.—J. BALL.
A Celebrated Golf Ball.

A cigarette card from 'Copes Golfers' series showing John Ball. He was the first Englishman to win the Open: for the previous fifty years it had been dominated by Scotsmen.

Author of *The Complete Golfer* and famous for his grip, Vardon was the master stylist when it came to golf.

H. VARDON.

THE GRIP (H. VARDON).

Vardon won the Open in 1896, 1898, 1899, 1903, 1911 and 1914. He was runner-up in 1900, 1901, 1902 and 1912. He became the American Open Champion in 1900. Unfortunately, most of his impressive collection of medals were stolen in 1908. The two cards above come from Churchman's 1927 series of fifty called 'Famous Golfers'.

CHURCHMAN'S CIGARETTES

HARRY VARDON

Vardon caricatured in around 1930 – this card is twelfth in Churchman's 'Prominent Golfers' series.

Tom Morris.   Harry Vardon.   Alexr. Herd (Champion 1902).

Open Championship.

Action from a St Andrews Open match (probably 1905, when Vardon finished ninth).

H. VARDON

Harry Vardon was born in Jersey on 9 May 1870 and died on 20 March 1937. He was part of the triumvirate, along with Taylor and Braid, who dominated British golf for over twenty years.

VARDON PITCHING

Postcard, *c.* 1908. Renowned for his stylish play, Vardon was unequalled in hitting brassie shots close to the flag.

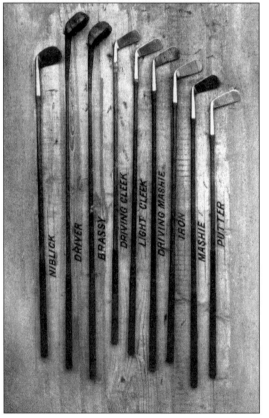

NIBLICK DRIVER BRASSY DRIVING CLEEK LIGHT CLEEK DRIVING MASHIE IRON MASHIE PUTTER

The golf clubs of Harry Vardon – one can only speculate what value these would have in today's market!

Right: This postcard of Arthur Balfour, the captain of the R&A in 1894, was sent in 1904. Balfour was Prime Minister of Great Britain from 1902 until 1906. He won the Parliamentary Golf Handicap in 1894 and 1897.

Bottom left: Taken from 'Copes Golfers' cigarette cards. *Bottom right:* No. 75 of 150 from the 'A' Series of Ogdens Tabs.

8.—A. J. BALFOUR.
" Putting the most trying to the Nerves."

RT. HON. ARTHUR BALFOUR.

OGDEN'S CIGARETTES

Leslie Balfour Melville represented Scotland not only at golf but also at cricket for over thirty years. At one time he was also the Scottish tennis champion and in 1872 he played rugby for Scotland against England. This photograph shows the Grange Cricket Club of Edinburgh on 13 July 1900. Balfour-Melville is the man seated with an umbrella. Other members of the R&A included A.G.G. Asher (back row third from left) and C.J.L. Boyd, (seated second from left).

Mr Leslie Balfour Melville winning Medal. (Record score—78.)
Famous Golfers. Valentine's Series

Born in 1854, Leslie Balfour Melville was a prominent member of the R&A for many years, becoming captain in 1906. He won his first tournament in 1874 and then took the King's Medal for the next three years. A winner of thirty-one R&A medals, the Jubilee Vase and many other trophies, he won the Amateur Championship at St Andrews in 1895.

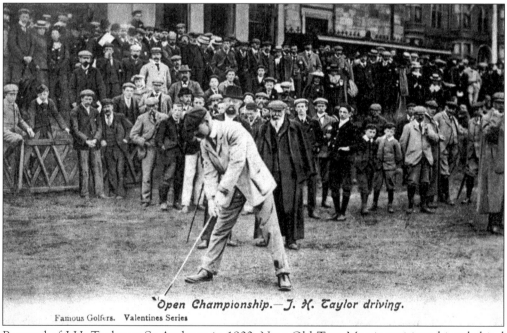

Open Championship.—J. H. Taylor driving.
Famous Golfers. Valentines Series

Postcard of J.H. Taylor at St Andrews in 1900. Note Old Tom Morris positioned just behind Taylor.

22.—J. H. TAYLOR.

Open Champion 1894-5.

A St Andrews Open champion in 1895 and 1900, this cigarette card comes from 'Cope's Golfers' 1900 series.

J.H. Taylor, a double winner of St Andrew Opens. This feat was only ever achieved by three others; Bob Martin (1876 and 1885), James Braid (1895 and 1900) and Jack Nicklaus (1970 and 1978). Pictured here are cigarette cards of Taylor from various manufacturers.

28.—PROFESSOR TAIT.
Theory of Golf.

Professor Tait, the father of Freddie, was born in Dalkeith in 1831. He was educated at Edinburgh and Cambridge Universities, where he took the highest honours attainable. In 1854 he was appointed Professor of Mathematics at Queens College, Belfast. He returned to Edinburgh in 1860 as Professor of Natural Philosophy (i.e. Physics). His holidays were spent at St Andrews, where he said the air refreshed him for the term ahead. Professor Tait's love of golf was passed on to his children – Freddie Guthrie Tait being his third son.

Freddie Tait was born on 11 January 1870. When asked by the Tsar of Russia how he had become such an accomplished golfer, he is supposed to have replied, 'I took to it seriously when I was eight years old'.

Medal Play.—The late Mr F. G. Tait driving.

Tait competing in the St Andrews Medal in September 1894. A record score of 78 won him the King William IV Medal and also the Glennie Aggregate Medal for that year.

Tait was Amateur Champion in 1896 and 1898. In May 1899 he tied with John Ball over the thirty-six holes for the Championship but lost on the thirty-seventh with a score of four against Ball's three.

The finish of a medal round, September 1899. Tait won the Glennie Medal for the third time with a score of 163. This was possibly the last time he played St Andrews.

Lieutenant F.G. Tait in 1891. He was killed in action on 7 February 1900 while leading his men of the Black Watch in an attack on the Boers at Koodoosberg Drift.

A St Andrews man through and through, Willie Auchterlonie was an excellent golfer. The Open Champion of 1893, he was also honorary professional at St Andrews and a member of the R&A. His son Laurie became famous as a club maker.

W. AUCHTERLONIE

289 A   LORD ABERDEEN.   ROTARY PHOTO. E.C

Lord Aberdeen was a frequent visitor to the Old Course, being a member of the R&A. This postcard of him dates from around 1910.

87

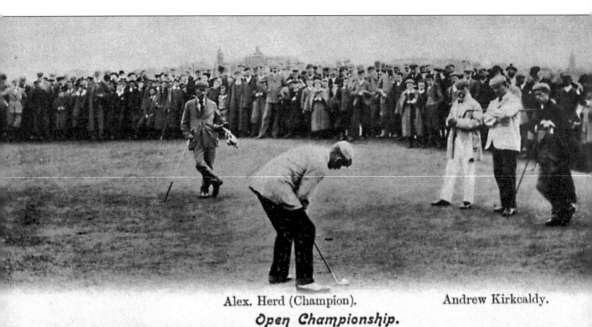

Alex. Herd (Champion).   Andrew Kirkcaldy.
Open Championship.

Famous Golfers. Valentines Series

The Open at St Andrews, 1900.

ALEX HERD

46.—ALEX. HERD.

Alex Herd won his only Open at Hoylake in 1902, beating Vardon and Braid by one shot. Andrew Kirkaldy (note the incorrect spelling on the postcard at the top of the page) was a St Andrews' club professional from 1910 to 1933.

St Andrews Open of 1936. On the left is Alex Herd and on the right Jack White, the 1904 Open Champion.

WILLS'S CIGARETTES.

ALEXANDER HERD.

ALEX HERD

Two more collectable cigarette cards of the great man, Alexander (Sandy) Herd, who was born in St Andrews in 1868 and died in London during 1944. Though a fabulous golfer, the Open eluded him for many years. His success in 1902 came partly through using the newly invented rubber-cored ball whilst others persevered with the gutta.

WILLS'S CIGARETTES.

EDWARD RAY.

Ted Ray finished eleventh at the St Andrews Open of 1905. He finally became Open Champion in 1912.

Ted Ray was the American Open Champion in 1920. One of the games most popular characters, he was instantly recognisable on the St Andrews links because of his constant pipe smoking and trilby hat. This picture is courtesy of G.B. and T.W. Cards – this being fourteenth in a series of twenty called 'Golfing Greats'.

EDWARD RAY

From left to right: James Braid, Harry Vardon, Edward 'Ted' Ray.

This card is thirty-fifth in Churchman's 'Famous Golfers' series of fifty cards, issued in 1927.

Two limited edition telephone cards produced from 1900 postcards.

These cards help to show how even today postcards issued nearly 100 years ago can still be of use.

Eight

Between the Wars

Duncan was born at Methlick, Aberdeenshire, in 1883. At one time he simultaneously held the record at three championship links – Westward Ho! (70), Sandwich (69) and, more importantly, St Andrews (68). Duncan won the Open at Deal in 1920. No championships were held between 1915 and 1919, but to celebrate the end of the First World War a tournament called the Professional Golfer's Championship was held at St Andrews. Duncan tied for first place with Abe Mitchell but lost out when they agreed to decide the championship on the result of their scores in the next day's Eden Tournament. This card is ninth in the 'Famous Golfers' set of 50 cards by W.A. & A.C. Churchman. Duncan is shown here using the Vardon overlapping grip when playing a spoon shot.

WALTER HAGEN

WILLS'S CIGARETTES.

WALTER J. HAGEN.

Top left: Walter Hagen with the Open Championship Cup, which he won on four occasions. Anyone who witnessed the St Andrews Open of 1921 would never have forgotten the sight of Walter Hagen resplendent in white shirt, black bow-tie, black and white diamond stockings and striped plus-fours. *Top right*: Number twenty-seven of Millhoff's 1928 'Famous Golfers' series. *Bottom left*: Number seven in Will's 'Famous Golfers' series of 1930.

Jim Barnes, a native of Cornwall, emigrated to USA in 1905. At the St Andrews Open of 1921 he finished sixth. He was the Open Champion at Prestwick in 1925.

CHURCHMAN'S CIGARETTES.

J. BARNES (U.S.A.).

WILLS'S CIGARETTES.

HAROLD D. GILLIES.

Harold Gillies was a famous surgeon who invented a very high tee (twelve inches long), but the Royal and Ancient indicated that they did not think this was in accord with the traditions of the game. Gillies won the Silver Medal at St Andrews in the spring of 1928.

ROGER H. WETHERED

R. H. WETHERED

Roger Wethered, a member of the R&A, in the 1921 Open final at St Andrews; he tied on 296 with Jock Hutchinson but lost the play-off. In the Walker Cup match at St Andrews in 1923, Wethered and Tolley had a famous victory over Ouimet and Sweetser by six and five.

Dai Rees

2 IMPACT

1 CLUB
TAKEN BACK

3 END OF STROKE

STYMIE
Note how face of club is opened at end of back-swing.

Dai Rees was a fantastic Welsh golfer who unfortunately never won an Open. St Andrews in 1939 saw him finish twelfth, seven behind the winner.

A. Compston was one golfer who didn't play at St Andrews as, coming over for the Open of 1927, he suffered so badly with flu he was unable to compete.

CHURCHMAN'S CIGARETTES.

A. COMPSTON.

CHURCHMAN'S CIGARETTES.

J. SWEETSER (U.S.A.).

An American Amateur Champion in 1922, Sweetser played in every Walker Cup contest from 1922 until 1928 and again in 1932. Possibly his best match was at St Andrews in 1926 when he defeated Sir E. Holderness by four and three. Born in 1893, he was a giant of a man who first came to prominence in the Gleneages tournament of 1922 where he reached the semi-final. In the 1933 Open at St Andrews, Sweetser was playing with Henry Cotton when the Prince of Wales appeared. Having previously played extremely well, he began to show off and his tournament went downhill from then on.

CHURCHMAN'S CIGARETTES.

A. G. HAVERS.

Born in 1898, A.G. Havers first qualified for the Open when only sixteen, finally becoming Open Champion in 1923.

Gallaher's Cigarettes

T.M.BERNELL.

An enthusiastic amateur, T.M. Bernell enjoyed playing St Andrews whenever time allowed him to leave his farm. He was the Scottish Amateur Champion in 1923.

Born in Kirkcaldy in 1898, A.F. Simpson learned most of his golf in the Highlands of Scotland. He reached the final of the British Amateur Championship of 1926 (but was defeated by Jess Sweetser) and played for Scotland against England in 1927 and Ireland in 1928. He was reported to have been an extremely powerful driver.

Few better golfers have come out of Glasgow than William Campbell. Born 4 July 1900, he was a Scottish international player who represented his country against Ireland seven times, England eight times and Wales four times. He represented Great Britain in the Walker Cup match of 1930 and in the same year reached the fifth round of the Amateur Championship held at St Andrews.

CHURCHMAN'S CIGARETTES

HARRISON R. JOHNSTON

Born in 1897, 'Jimmie' Johnston was one of America's most popular golfers. He was regarded as first choice for the Walker Cup matches of 1923, 1924, 1928 and 1930. Both cards on this page are from Churchman's 'Prominent Golfers' series of 1931.

CHURCHMAN'S CIGARETTES

SIR E. W. E. HOLDERNESS, BART.

Sir E.W.E. Holderness made a very strong challenge for the Amateur Championship at St Andrews in 1930 and reached the sixth round before going out to Bobby Jones on the eighteenth. He won the British Amateur Championship in 1922 and 1924.

Rex Hartley was a member of the Walker Cup team in 1930 and 1932. An injury to his right shoulder while still at school meant that he was essentially a left arm player. He was considered to have been one of the best amateur players up to the green and played for England against Scotland on numerous occasions, including at St Andrews in 1930 when he helped England to victory.

WILLS'S CIGARETTES.

REX W. HARTLEY.

CHURCHMAN'S CIGARETTES

R. MACKENZIE

Ronald Mackenzie, an American amateur of Scottish extraction, was only nineteen when he helped the USA beat Britain in the Walker Cup match at St Andrews in 1926. He played at St Andrews in the 1930 Amateur Championship but failed to achieve the standard he had set himself on his own side of the Atlantic.

WILLS'S CIGARETTES.

T. HENRY COTTON.

Born in 1907, Henry Cotton became a professional at the age of seventeen and won his first Open in 1934, having finished seventh at St Andrews in 1933.

GOLF - HENRY COTTON

After the war Cotton went on to become one of the greatest golfers of all time. He once said of St Andrews, 'The Old Course is different from any other course and is sometimes an acquired taste for newcomers'.

Lawson Little was the pride of American golf in the mid-1930s. In the 1934 Amateur Championship final he beat James Walker (Troon) by fourteen up with thirteen to play. Similarly, at the St Andrews Walker Cup match of 1934 he beat Tolley by seven and five. This is the twentieth card in G.B. and T.W. Cards' 'Golfing Greats' series.

LAWSON LITTLE

GOLF - W. LAWSON LITTLE, U.S.A.

Born in Fort Adams (Newport, USA) in 1910, he followed Bobby Jones with his British successes, winning both the 1934 and 1935 Amateur Championship. As much as he liked playing St Andrews, his best Open placing on the course was tenth. The card is from J.A. Pattreiouex's 'Sporting Events and Stars' series and is twenty-first in a set of ninety-six.

103

A British Amateur Open Champion at the age of twenty-two, Hector Thomson beat the Australian Jim Ferrier by two holes at St Andrews in 1936. This is a card from the set by W.D. & H.O. Wills titled, 'British Sporting Personalities'.

The St Andrews Open Championship of 1936, with the winner Hector Thomson on the right and, beside him, the runner-up Jim Ferrier. The photograph was taken at the side of the R&A clubhouse – note the Martyrs Monument in the background.

Cecil Ewing playing the first at St Andrews. Reginald Cecil Ewing was from Rosses Point in Ireland and won many Irish tournaments. He represented the Emerald Isle for over twenty years from 1934 onwards and was runner-up to C.R. Yates in the Amateur Championship of 1938. In the great St Andrews Walker Cup match of 1938, Ewing beat Ray Billows by one hole.

Robert Harris was Amateur Champion in 1925 and runner-up at St Andrews in 1913, winning the Royal St George Cup in 1905 and 1920, also tying for the trophy in 1906 with S. Mure Ferguson (losing the replay). He won the Gold Vase in 1911 and 1912 and played in both the St Andrews Walker Cup matches of 1923 and 1926.

The 1938 Walker Cup team pictured outside the R&A. From left to right, back row: Gordon Peters, Hector Thomson, Leonard Crawley, Alex Kyle, Frank Pennick. Front row: Harry Bentley, Cecil Ewing, John Beck, Charles Stowe, Jimmy Bruen.

Sixteen years had passed since the competition's inception on Long Island, USA, and 1938 saw a resounding victory for the Great Britain team. The American team in 1938 consisted of, from left to right: Marvin Ward, Fred Haas, Charles Yates, John Goodman, John Fischer, Ray Billows, Charles Kocsis, Reynold Smith.

Nine

Bobby Jones

Bobby Jones leaping over the Swilken Burn. (Photograph courtesy of St Andrews Preservation Trust Museum.)

R. T. JONES (U.S.A.).

Bernard Darwin wrote of Bobby Jones: 'Like the man in the song, many of Jones' opponents are tired of living but feared of dying. However their fears are unduly protracted since they usually die very soon after lunch.'

Bobby Jones was born in Atlanta on 17 March 1902. The son of Robert Purmedus Jones and Clare Merrick Thomas (Jones) he weighed around five pounds at birth and his chances of survival were slim – his 'elder' brother, who had been of similar health, died aged three months. He received the Freedom of the Burgh of St Andrews on 9 October 1958 and is quoted as saying 'I could take out my life everything except my experience of St Andrews and still have a rich life'.

GOLF - R. T. (BOBBY) JONES, U.S.A.

I wonder what Bobby Jones would do now ?

Jones had a genuine affection for the Old Course, being both a member of the R&A as well as his home club East Lake, Georgia. Here is another postcard featuring the great man, this one from around 1930.

CHURCHMAN'S CIGARETTES

BOBBY JONES

This is the fifth card in a series called 'Prominent Golfers' issued by Churchmans cigarettes. When Bobby Jones retired in 1930 he had won thirteen major tournaments in the previous eight years.

Bobby Jones with the Amateur Championship Cup, which he won at St Andrews in 1930.

Jones putting on the eighteenth green while competing in the 1930 Amateur Championship. This was possibly his finest season.

Tragically, Jones suffered in later years from syringomyelia, a crippling disease which resulted in the loss of the use of his arms and legs, and he died in Atlanta on 8 December 1971.

Bobby Jones at the final tee in the British Open at St Andrews 1927, waiting for the marshalls to clear the fairways, before going on to win the Championship.

At the first tee in 1921, playing out of the whins at the turn.

Ten
The Ladies

ST. ANDREWS FROM THE LINKS

In the publication *The Gentleman's Book of Sports*, a lady who played golf was described as being 'a fast and almost disreputable person, definitely one to be avoided'.

Postcard, *c.* 1906. Horace Hutchison, a great golfer, wrote in 1893 that 'constitutionally and physically women are unfitted for golf'. How wrong could he be!

32.—LADY MARGARET SCOTT.

At only eighteen years of age, Lady Margaret Scott won her first British Championship in 1893. Lady Margaret spent nearly all her holidays at St Andrews and as a youngster often partnered Andrew Kirkaldy around the course.

One of the finest women golfers ever born, Joyce Wethered was winner of the Ladies Open in 1922, 1924 and 1925, and then came out of retirement to triumph again in 1929.

WILLS'S CIGARETTES.

MISS JOYCE WETHERED.

CHURCHMAN'S CIGARETTES

MISS JOYCE WETHERED

It was at St Andrews in 1929 that she won her fourth Ladies Open when she defeated Miss Collett (USA) by three and one in what was amongst the greatest finishes of all time.

Runner-up in the 1929 Ladies Open at St Andrews, Miss G. Collett was an outstanding US golfer and five times American Champion.

Born in Glasgow in 1907, Mrs A.M. Holm played most of her early golf around St Andrews. It was often said her swing had 'many characteristics of St Andrews'. She was Scottish champion on many occasions from 1930 onwards. This cigarette card was produced by Stephen Mitchell & Son in their series 'A Gallery of 1935'.

To quote from Cecil Leitch's *Golf for Girls*: 'At St Andrews on the occasion of my first championship in 1908, I carried nine clubs, but no duplicates. Experience has taught me the unwisdom of not carrying duplicates.' This book was published in 1923.

Cecil Leitch won her first Open title in 1914 and retained her title in 1920 and 1921 (the war having intervened to prevent more Open successes). However, she does have the distinction of holding the title for the longest period, from 1914 to 1921 – a good pub quiz question. The photograph is from a postcard of around 1916. This postcard occasionally turns up in postcard dealers' boxes of 'actresses' – little do they know.

Action from the Scottish Ladies final of 1911. The winner, Miss E. Grant Suttie, is the player putting, whilst the runner-up is I.L. Kyle. These pictures do turn up as postcards and are extremely rare.

The Ladies Golf Championship at St Andrews in 1908. (Both the pictures on this page are courtesy of the St Andrews Preservation Trust Museum.)

Eleven

And so to Rest

This recent photograph was taken from just outside the walls of St Andrews Cathedral. Many famous golfers have been laid to rest here and the following pages will show a few of these resting places. The tall building to the left in the photograph is the gable end of what was the large cathedral built in the twelfth century. If you look closely at the bottom of this tower you may just see Young Tom Morris's memorial in the far wall.

At the top and to the right-hand side of the above photograph is the church of St Regulus (St Rule). The church dates from around 1130 but only the tower and choir remain. To the left can be seen the gable end of the cathedral. Both of the pictures on this page are from postcards, the top one issued around 1908 and the one below around 1940.

S 2390. St. Andrews Cathedral.

This shows the memorial to Young Tom, while all around are others to members of his family.

This tombstone is just in front of the memorial. Note that Tommy (Young Tom) had a younger brother also named Thomas. Below this is Old Tom's grave.

This very rare and unusual postcard shows the Tom Morris Memorial Bronze which is located on the west front of the R&A clubhouse. Designed by W.H. Paton, the memorial was subscribed for by golf clubs and individual golfers. The R&A contributed £100 towards the cost.

A memorial to Allan Robertson, with the last line of the text reading, 'To the champion golfer of Scotland'. Robertson was born in St Andrews in 1815 and was said never to have been beaten in any individual stake match. He died in 1858, two years before the Open was instigated. His memorial is situated almost in the middle of the cathedral grounds.

The grave of Andrew Kirkaldy (1880-1934) in the Eastern Cemetery, close to where Andrew Lang lies buried.

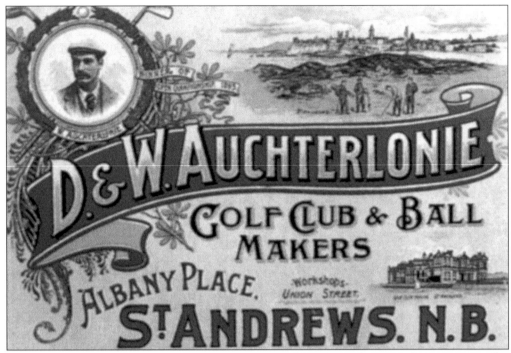

The Auchterlonies are renowned as golf club makers. Perhaps the most famous was Willie Auchterlonie, who won the Open in 1893. You don't have to look far to find gravestones with this family's name on them.

Erected by his father, this is the gravestone of Andrew Strath, who was 1865 Open Champion.

Alex Herd, who was the Open Champion in 1902, was known as a real St Andrews man and his grave is located in the Eastern Cemetery.

What a family! The Blackwells were famous for their golfing abilities. Amongst their achievements was Walter Blackwell's winning of the R&A Victoria Jubilee in 1896 and James Hay Blackwell's triumph in the Bombay Medal of 1881. Ernley Blackwell was Under-Secretary of State in 1909, having won the R&A Gold Medal in 1892 and the St George's Vase in 1895.

The brother of Andrew, Hugh Kirkaldy was Open Champion in 1891, winning the competition in his home town of St Andrews. Tragically, he died from consumption at the young age of twenty-nine.

A postcard from around 1900. Is that Old Tom at the left-hand side of the three old men? He appears to have a golf club in his hand.

Postcard showing the graveyard (bottom left), *c.* 1910. 'The Links' are to the right just beyond the buildings. See page 12 to compare the view from the north. Is there a more peaceful resting place?

A final reminder of how fit golfers must be. This sixty-two page book deals with the physical side of improving your game. It was written in 1936 by Lieutenant A. Stark of the Department of Physical Training at the University of St Andrews.